G000144783

WITNESS

WITNESS

The Faith and Order Commission
of the Church of England

CHURCH HOUSE
PUBLISHING

Church House Publishing
Church House
Great Smith Street
London SW1P 3AZ
www.chpublishing.co.uk

Published 2020 for the Faith and Order Commission
of the Church of England by Church House Publishing

Copyright © The Archbishops' Council 2020

ISBN 978 0 7151 1173 4   (Paperback)
ISBN 978 0 7151 1174 1   (CoreSource eBook)
ISBN 978 0 7151 1175 8   (Kindle eBook)

GS Misc 1253

All rights reserved. Other than copies for local,
non-commercial use by dioceses or parishes
in the Church of England, no part of this publication
may be reproduced or stored or transmitted by
any means or in any form, electronic or mechanical,
including photocopying, recording, or any information
storage and retrieval system, without written permission
which should be sought from the Copyright
Administrator, The Archbishops' Council (address
above). E-mail: copyright@churchofengland.org

Unless otherwise indicated, the Scripture quotations
contained herein are from the New Revised Standard
Version, © 1989, 1995 by the Division of Christian
Education of the National Council of the Churches
of Christ in the USA, and are used with permission.
All rights reserved.

British Library Cataloguing in Publication Data

A catalogue record for this book is available
from the British Library

Typeset by ForDesign

Printed and bound by CPI Group (UK) Ltd, Croydon, CR0 4YY

Contents

Preface

For some years, the Faith and Order Commission has been thinking about witness as a rich theological theme with many resonances for the Church of England at the present time. As this report sets out, witness requires a readiness to speak of what we have seen and heard, but also to point away from ourselves and to listen with humility to others as we learn how to communicate the truth entrusted to us by Jesus Christ, who calls us to be his witnesses in the localities into which each of us is placed (Acts 1.8).

The report constitutes something of a new departure for the Commission. Well over half the text comprises a set of case studies, based on visits to eight different church communities and interviews with those involved in them. The relative brevity of the first Part and the opening section of the third, where the Commission speaks as it were in its own voice, should not be mistaken for a lack of weight or depth. Between them, space has been deliberately given for a range of distinctive and varied voices to articulate their own account of what it means to be God's witnesses in their particular situations.

Many people have contributed to this text. As well as members and staff of the Commission during this period, Anne Richards has provided valuable support and has been an important link with the Mission Theology Advisory Group. I am deeply grateful to those from the church communities in the eight case studies who were so generous in sharing their experiences, and to Muthuraj Swamy, Hannah Lewis and Martyn Snow for providing their reflections. None of this would have been possible without Mike Higton's leadership of the project and the many gifts and skills he has brought to it, and the Commission is very much in his debt for this.

My hope is that the report we are now publishing will strengthen the church in being – to use the words of the 1930 Lambeth Conference – 'a fellowship of witness' in the time and place where God has set us.

Christopher Cocksworth
Bishop of Coventry
Chair, Faith and Order Commission

How to use this book

It is sometimes said that Church of England reports have a short shelf life, but for some of them the opposite is no less true: they end up sitting on a shelf, their spines gently fading, making no difference to anybody.

This report has a different purpose and we hope it will find a different use. It is intended to offer a picture of the great joy of Christian witness in the world, to help readers imagine how they and their churches might witness more richly, and to inspire readers to put what they have imagined into action. Read it, yes, but read it with intention, asking, 'How are we going to respond to this?'

To help you address that question, at the end of each of the three Parts that follow you will find some material for discussion and reflection. It includes invitations to 'immerse', 'inhabit', 'imagine' and 'experiment'. You could use it to help you as an individual to digest what you're reading as you go along. This is not simply a report for individual readers, however. It is also one for church communities. Witness is not something that we do in isolation from others, and the case studies in Part 2 show how, in their very different contexts, a wide range of church communities are seeking to be God's witnesses together. We therefore hope that you might want to study this report together with others, perhaps in your own church, or as a PCC, or with people from other churches. You could use it as the basis for three separate, shorter sessions or tackle the material from all three Parts in a single day.

At the end, you'll find an invitation to share what you've learnt more widely. We want to hear from you, and to be able to share more stories of the different forms that witness takes around the church. We want what we have written here to be the nucleus of something that grows – not simply another report gathering dust on a shelf.

Introduction

In 1930, several hundred bishops from the worldwide Anglican Communion met for the 'Lambeth Conference'. In a letter written at the end of the conference they said,

> we have discovered one idea underlying all our long deliberations: it is the idea of *witness* ... the Church is called to bear witness to the supreme revelation of God ... which has been given to the world in Jesus Christ our Lord.[1]

In fact, they said, 'it would be a true description of the Church of Christ to say that it is a fellowship of witness'.

Much more recently, 'witness' has been one of the themes stressed by the current Archbishop of Canterbury, Justin Welby. On the Church of England web page that sets this out as one of his priorities, we read that

> Every follower of Christ has witnessed for themselves the abundant love that God has for them, and every one of us is sent in the power of the Holy Spirit to live lives and speak words which tell of that. We do this so that friends and family, colleagues and neighbours can themselves come to witness first hand the goodness of God's transforming love for them.[2]

This report from the Faith and Order Commission is an exploration of what this idea of 'witness' means in the life of the church. It is not a report that makes detailed recommendations for policy and practice, nor does it address a particular controversy. It is, instead, intended as a theological resource – a reflection on a theme that matters for the life of the whole church. We hope to encourage all God's people to think of themselves as witnesses, and we hold up some examples that might inspire us all to go further in our witness together.

We believe that thinking about 'witness' can help us make sense of the life of the church, and the life of each individual Christian, in the world. It can give us a set of ideas to explore, a set of patterns to look for, and a set of questions to pose.

In **Part 1** of this report, we explore some of these ideas, patterns, and questions, under three headings: 'Seeing, hearing and saying', 'Pointing away', and 'Learning to communicate'.

In **Part 2**, we describe a series of practical case studies, which show some of the ways in which witness is happening across the Church of England today.

In **Part 3**, we gather a set of further reflections on witness in the church, prompted by these case studies.

We hope that, together, these materials will enrich people's imaginations, spark their creativity, and help the witness of the church to grow.

Part 1: WHAT IS WITNESS?

Seeing, hearing and saying

The webpage mentioned above says that 'A witness is someone who simply says ... what they have seen and heard for themselves.' The first thing to note about this definition is that, for witnesses, the *seeing and hearing* come before the *saying*.

'Seeing and hearing' aren't restricted to our literal eyes and ears. They involve all of our senses, and all of our understanding – the whole process by which we notice what God is doing, and are captivated by it. '*Hear*, O Israel!', 'O *taste* and *see* that the Lord is good!' 'We declare to you ... what we have ... *touched* with our hands, concerning the word of life'; 'thanks be to God, who ... spreads in every place the *fragrance* that comes from knowing him', 'so that ... all may *consider and understand*, that the hand of the Lord has done this'.[3]

Whether they are literal or metaphorical, however, this seeing and hearing come first. Before we say or do anything, becoming a witness is something that happens to us.

Think of Moses in the desert, tending his father-in-law's flock:

> There the angel of the Lord appeared to him in a flame of fire out of a bush; he looked, and the bush was blazing, yet it was not consumed. Then Moses said, 'I must turn aside and look at this great sight.[4]

His attention is caught by something, his curiosity aroused, and so he turns aside to look more closely. It is then that he is given the role of speaking about God in the world, and of accompanying that speaking with action. That role is based on what he has seen, and on his turning aside to look more closely.

Or think of the women who went early on the first Easter morning to Jesus' tomb, to tend to his dead body.

> They found the stone rolled away from the body, but when they went in, they did not find the body. While they were perplexed about this, suddenly two men in dazzling clothes stood beside them. The women were terrified and bowed their faces to the ground, but the men said to them, 'Why do you look for the living among the dead? He is not here, but has risen.'[5]

The women were made witnesses because of what they unexpectedly found – and what they still more unexpectedly did not find. And on that basis they were commissioned to spread the good news. They were asked to bear witness. The whole Christian church through history is the gathering of those added to the community of these women: the community of witnesses.

To focus on witness means placing our own action in second place. Our action emerges from what we have seen and heard – from what we have been shown and told; what we have found.

The message of the women at the tomb, and of the other witnesses whom God has added to their number, reaches us through Scripture. It reaches us through the worship in which we learn to inhabit the story they passed on. It reaches us through experiences of the Spirit working in the life of the church to lead us deeper into the truth of this story.

All the stories of witness that we tell in the case studies below are stories that involve people who have been shown something in this way: who have been fed by Scripture, shaped by worship, and led by the Spirit.

There is a second sense, though, in which they are stories of seeing and hearing before they are stories of doing. In different ways, each of them is a story of people who pay attention to the world around them. With ears and eyes shaped by all that they have been learning about God, they look closely at the people and situations around them. They look for the opportunities, the resources, the gifts, the challenges that God has placed in their path. They listen out for the sound of God already at work in the lives of those they meet. They see the work of God, blazing unexpectedly beside their path.

The work of witness is never simply our own initiative. It is always a response. It depends completely on what we have received and go on receiving, on what we have been shown and told and go on being shown and told, and on what we have learnt and go on learning.

Pointing away

When the Archbishop of Canterbury's 'Evangelism and Witness' webpage expands on its initial definition ('A witness is someone who simply says … what they have seen and heard for themselves'), it doesn't offer a description of Christian activity. Instead, it focuses our attention on God. It says that 'Every follower of Christ has witnessed for themselves the abundant love that God has for them.'[6]

Our activity as witnesses is not meant to draw people's attention to ourselves, but to point people to God, to what God has done, to God's work in their lives, and to God's work in the world around them.

Christian witness could be thought of as joining in the song described in Psalm 96. In words and deeds, we 'tell of God's salvation from day to day' and 'Declare God's glory among the nations, God's marvellous works among all the peoples.' If we want to ask how successful our witness is, its success will be measured by how well it sings that song – how richly, how fully, how compellingly it points people to God and God's work.

That is why witness and worship are intimately knotted together. In worship, we turn our attention toward the God who meets us in Jesus. We face toward God in gratitude, adoration and delight, and in penitence, lament, and petition. In witness, we draw others' attention in the same direction – calling them to look where we are looking. Worship makes witness possible; witness leads back to worship; and worship is itself a form of witness.

Witness therefore involves a balancing act. The people amongst whom we witness notice us – they see us and hear us – only in order to be pointed away from us. If our witnessing doesn't attract any attention, it cannot be effective, but if it remains the focus of attention, it is not witness.

We see this balancing act in the interplay between witness's multiple dimensions. The 'Evangelism and Witness' webpage says that 'every one of us is sent in the power of the Holy Spirit to live lives and speak words' which tell of what we have seen and heard – and witness is a matter of lives and words, working together.

Witness is a matter of *showing* the love of God to those around us. It is a matter of living in a way that shows that we believe the story of God's gracious love to be true. It is a matter of living in a way that communicates something of that love to others.

It is also a matter of *telling* people of that love, which is always deeper and wider than anything we in our faltering love manage to show. We tell the story of a love greater than ours, a love on which we depend.

It is a matter of *upholding* the good news of God's love in contexts where its existence and power are denied – of calling others (and ourselves) out of the unloving patterns of our lives.

It is a matter of *celebrating* all the places and the faces in which we find that love at work, all the occasions on which that love surprises us, appearing where we had least expected it.

It is a matter of *acknowledging* that all our witnessing fails to do justice to its source, and pointing people to the God upon whose gracious judgment, forgiveness, and teaching we depend.

It is a matter of *learning* to witness more fully, more truly – including from those amongst whom we witness, through whom God can show God's gracious love to us in new ways.

It is a matter of *trusting* God to be God's own witness, despite all our failures. God is at work by God's Spirit, drawing people to Jesus, and though we are called to participate in that work, God's loving grace is also at work before, apart from, and after anything we might do.

Our witness involves all these dimensions, interacting with one another and qualifying one another. It is not one simple activity, confined to one part of the lives we lead as followers of Jesus. It is one way of seeing the whole shape of those lives.

Learning to communicate

At the end of his life, Joshua erected a stone in the sanctuary at Shechem as a witness – a standing reminder of God's covenant with God's people.[7] Witness can take the form of an event, an interruption, a cry: an intervention in a particular situation that calls attention to God's gracious love and the demands that it makes. And witness can also take the form of a steady presence, a faithful persistence, like that of a standing stone.

Yet even when it takes the form of a surprising intervention, witness cannot be a hit-and-run affair. In John 6, we see a moment of misrecognition. A large crowd is following Jesus, 'because they saw the signs that he was doing for the sick', and they try to 'take him by force to make him king'.[8] They make sense of Jesus within their existing expectations, and so mistake the kind of king he is. That is perhaps why Jesus repeatedly instructed people not to spread the news that he was the Messiah.[9] Anyone in his culture who was simply told that message was bound to get the wrong idea, because they would not yet have the language, the expectations, that would allow them to hear what it really meant. There was therefore, for most people, no quick way for Jesus to share this message with them. They needed to spend time with him, to hear his words and see his actions, to follow his story through, in order to make sense of him.

We can't witness without developing together some kind of shared language that will allow us to communicate with one another. That is often a slow process, and one that requires attentiveness and sensitivity.

It can't happen if we don't pay close attention to the language, the patterns of life and understanding, of those amongst whom we are witnessing. And so we can't truly witness to people without spending time with them, and being drawn deeply into relationship with them.

That might sometimes mean that we invite people into encounter and engagement with us. It will also sometimes mean that we accept invitation into encounter and engagement with them. Sometimes it will simply mean a development of the relationships in which we already find ourselves, and it won't be clear who invited whom, or who is guest and who is host. We won't always – perhaps we won't even normally – be the hosts as we learn to witness.

One thing we can be sure about, though. Learning to witness is a process that will change us, perhaps far more than we expect. As we learn to communicate with others the love of God in word and action, we will learn to know that love in new ways – and we will become, once again, recipients. We will be drawn back to worship – to gratitude, adoration, and delight, and to penitence, lament, and petition – as we receive the gift of God's love afresh from those amongst whom we are witnessing.

Conclusion

The church's witness can take many forms. There is no one template for what it will look like. It might take forms like Joshua's standing stone, like the Psalmist's song, like the women rushing from the empty tomb, or like Moses standing up before Pharaoh. It can be costly and dangerous: our word 'martyr' comes from the Greek word for 'witness', and in many contexts in history, and around the world today, upholding the good news has taken the form of martyrdom. It can also, however, be a matter of everyday words, habits and actions.

Witness can primarily take the form of proclaiming the Good News of the Kingdom. It can take the form of teaching, baptising and nurturing new believers. It can take the form of responding to human need by loving service. It can take the form of transforming the unjust structures of society, challenging violence of every kind, and pursuing peace and reconciliation. It can take the form of striving to safeguard the integrity of creation, and sustaining and renewing the life of the earth.[10]

This might make it sound like everything in Christian life is witness – and if we say that everything is 'witness', the word will cease to name anything in particular. Witness is not, however, the name for one small domain of activity marked off from others, something that we might do from time to time, or that might be a task only for a few of us. Witness is an aspect of the whole of Christian life. What marks something out as witness is where it has come from, and where it points. Witness flows from what we have seen and heard, and what we go on seeing and hearing of God's work. And witness always points people away from us and towards God. It tells people of God, and helps them to see something more of God's nature and activity. Wherever we find that seeing and showing, that hearing and telling, we find witness.

All our witnessing takes place in relationship with those amongst whom God has called us to live – our friends and neighbours, our various communities and connections – and it always draws us deeper into those relationships, to see more and show more, hear more and tell more of the love of God. In the life of witness, we are all always both givers and receivers.

How are we going to respond?

Discussion: Bible study

Explore two or more biblical passages that speak about witness. Examples would include:

- Isaiah 43.8–13
- John 15.26–16.15
- Acts 1.1–11
- Acts 22.6–21
- Revelation 1.1–11.

Where in the passages you have looked at might you find some of the themes highlighted in the first Part of the report, with its three main headings of 'Seeing, hearing and saying', 'Pointing away' and 'Learning to communicate'?

Are there other themes or insights about witness that strike you in the passages you considered?

Reflection: Immerse

Pick out one of the scriptural references from Part 1 or from the passages listed above and simply live with it for a month. Inhabit that scripture and take it with you in your daily life. Use the scripture to listen to God more closely, to pray to God with more attention and listening. Think about how the scripture might open up and inform your own Christian witness.

Part 2: CASE STUDIES

This report combines general reflections on witness with descriptions of specific examples. The two elements belong together, and each informs the other. We have developed our thinking about witness as we explored a variety of practical examples; we explored those practical examples as we reflected together more generally on the nature of witness.

Witness takes place in individual lives, and in the actions of communities and institutions. It can take place in quiet personal interactions, or on a wide public stage. In this report, we focus on the publicly visible witness of communities and congregations. All of the case studies that follow are from particular English church contexts. Most of them are from parish churches, though there is one cathedral and one chaplaincy among them.

We don't pretend that these case studies cover the whole variety of witness that could be found if we looked more widely at the Church of England; still less do we think that they do justice to the wealth of witness that we could find if we looked at the wider Anglican Communion or the whole global church. These are local examples, all from one limited part of the church's life – and they are snapshots, capturing some of what was happening at one particular moment in time. We hope, nevertheless, that they are sufficiently different, and sufficiently interesting, to spark reflection on what witness might mean elsewhere.

We also don't pretend that these cover all the forms of witness in which Christians are involved, even in the contexts that we explore. We have, as we said, focused on the publicly visible witness of communities and congregations – on activities that were deliberately organised and pursued by the members of those communities and congregations, working together to witness to the world around them. Witness takes many other forms in Christians' individual lives, in their families and workplaces and friendships. That 'daily work and witness'[11] of Jesus' disciples is more the focus of another report, *Calling All God's People*, which could be thought of as a companion to this.[12]

We are not holding out the case studies we cover as templates to copy, or as ideals. These case studies are rich but imperfect, partial but exciting. We offer them simply as examples to think with, to help you reflect on what it might mean to explore more fully the possibilities of witness in your own local context.

1: Hodge Hill

In places like the Firs and Bromford estate in Birmingham, it is all too common for residents to be told that they have no value and no power, and that they have nothing to offer. What should the church's witness be in such a context? What can it look like amongst people who are too often made to feel that they are only ever the objects of others' concern, and the recipients of others' action?

For Al Barrett, the Rector of Hodge Hill, in the midst of this estate, it is very clear what should not happen. Witness should not mean that a bunch of people from outside this community come in to do things for those who live here. And witness should not mean that a group of people marked off from the wider community act as hosts and providers towards everyone else around them.

Paying attention, celebrating, and interpreting

The first thing that witness has to mean here is *paying attention to what God is doing in this community*. That means looking and listening for signs of God's kingdom – looking and listening for signs of the kind of life that God creates. It involves being present: being committed inhabitants of the place, spending time in the spaces where the life of this community happens, keeping eyes and ears wide open.

Witness also means *celebrating what God is doing in this community*. When signs of God's kingdom are seen, it means welcoming them, seeking to clear the way for them, holding them up for others to see, and expressing thanks for them to those involved. It also means giving thanks to God for all that is going on, and praying for God's kingdom to come still more visibly.

Witness also means *interpreting to the community what God is doing*. It means finding ways to offer to the community the news that the God of Jesus Christ is at work among them, and that this God has still more for them to discover. It means finding ways to name these signs of life as signs of God's kingdom, and inviting those involved to join in with prayer, thanksgiving and worship.

All of these – paying attention, celebrating, and interpreting – are certainly things that church people do. They do not, however, turn those amongst whom they are done into passive recipients. Instead, they are a form of 'hearing one another to speech':[13] a form of attention which recognises, encourages, and enables the growth of something that it does not produce or control.

In Hodge Hill, this takes various forms. For instance, there is a practice of 'street connecting'. Members of the community go door-to-door, introducing themselves to their neighbours, explaining that they are not there to sell or tell them anything, but asking them what they love about their community, what they would like to see change, and what they are passionate about that they could offer. The street connectors focus on harnessing the talents and resources that they find for local events and activities, for little hubs of community generated by the people who live there. They are driven by the belief that every one of their neighbours has value, and that every one of them has something to offer. They are witnesses, looking for the gifts that God has given and the work that God is doing in people's lives.

Another example is the weekly 'Open Door' drop-in session. This is a welcoming space, in which people meet to share food, to share company, and to help one another out. People might turn up initially as recipients, but they are quickly encouraged to get involved. They help keep the sessions running, prepare the food, and offer practical help to others who attend. Those who come end up being defined at least as much by what they can offer and what they bring as by what they need. The church here is not so much engaging in hospitality as in welcoming, enabling, and receiving the hospitality of others. The church is part of an emerging culture of gift-giving, in which everyone involved is able to be a giver as well as a recipient. People from the church are certainly involved in facilitating and enabling all this work – and it does take significant labour to keep these spaces open, to remove barriers to participation, and to respond to the difficulties that inevitably arise – but they are engaged in this work alongside many others, discovering together what is possible and what works. The life that flourishes in these spaces is generated by all those who participate.

The members of the church we spoke to described how they were seeing a deepening of authentic community. They were witnesses of people across the estate making more connections with their neighbours, of those connections deepening into friendships, of a growth in care and kindness. And 'growth' is an appropriate word: 'Caring is catching!', they said. People on the fringes of this activity see that something good is happening, something home-grown, and they are drawn deeper in. One person we spoke to said that there is kindness everywhere, but that here in Firs and Bromford they look for it, they value it, they celebrate it, they recognise that it is God's work – and 'it just grows'.

As that last comment suggests, as well as by paying attention and by celebrating, the church witnesses by interpreting what is happening. The people we spoke to were clear that they are seeing the God of Jesus Christ at work. They are captivated by the glimpses they catch of God's kingdom life emerging in this place. They have a strong sense that God has placed them there as witnesses, to see what God is up to. And they are clear that the God they are reading about in the Scriptures and praising in their worship – the God of Jesus Christ – is the same God who they are meeting at work in the lives around them.

The need for gentleness

To witness in this way, drawing people's attention to the way that God is already at work in their midst, requires gentleness. The growing web of relationships would be betrayed if Christians were thought to be trying to take it over, or take all the credit for it, or assume leadership of it. On the other hand, those relationships have also generated enough trust, enough friendship, to allow the Christians involved to speak their conviction that God is at work. And they have helped create a context in which that speaking can make sense.

So, for instance, one of the things happening on the estate is the Real Junk Food Kitchen, which now welcomes more than a hundred people every week to enjoy meals made from food that would otherwise be thrown away by shops and restaurants. The Kitchen is run by the community for the community, and it operates on a 'pay-as-you-feel' basis, for people paying in money or in kind or by volunteering to help. Those meals have now, quite naturally, ended up being followed by a time for prayer, in which participants – some of whom would identify as church people, and many others of whom would not – offer thanks to God for the good that is happening, and pray about all the things that still concern them. Their thankfulness to all involved and their dependence upon one another's help is gathered up in thankfulness to God and in asking God for help.

The church witnesses by interpreting what is going on, and by inviting others to acknowledge and respond to the God of Jesus Christ who is at work. But they can only do that because they have been looking and listening to what God is doing in their community. They can be people who speak only because they were first people who looked and listened, and then people who got involved.

2: Lewes

Lewes is a town of steep hills and tight twittens (narrow paths and passages) in the midst of the South Downs. It is a town with its own personality. Trinity Church holds services in three locations scattered around the town. It is not in the geographical centre, but it finds its way into the heart of the community's life.

Jules Middleton, the Associate Vicar, sees Trinity as a community of Christians living in the midst of Lewes who are committed to seeing their own lives and the lives of all around them transformed by the love of Christ. Each person is a unique creation, made and loved by God, and God's love in Christ can bring each person fully alive. Jules wants the church to be a space in which each person can grow and thrive, and can have their talents and gifts enabled, released, and welcomed.

The first thing you are likely to encounter when visiting the Trinity Centre is Café12/31. That's because it is just through the front doors, which are open enticingly wide, and because you can hear the chatter of customers as soon as you start walking up the path. Café12/31 has been designed to be open to anybody and everybody, and it is increasingly being used as a meetup place for people who don't normally come anywhere near the church's worship. People come because of the food and drinks available (on a par with anything you would find on the high street), and because of the beauty of the space. Jules thinks, though, that they also come because of the café's ethos. The name comes from Mark 12:31, Jesus' call to love our neighbours, and the whole project is run as an act of welcoming love. Staff try to treat the customers with friendly consideration, and to look out for their regulars. Jules spends time there meeting people. It is a space for making connections.

The second thing you might encounter at Trinity is music. There are several groups which work to create harmony – literally – in Lewes. Like Café12/31, the quality is high, especially the music created by LSG (Lewes Sings Gospel), who put on regular concerts, but that is not all that the musical projects are about. Rather, like the café, the choirs are intended to provide spaces that are part of the life of the church, but that are not restricted to those who already see themselves as part of that life. They are spaces next door to worship: spaces in which relationships can form, in which people can find a haven from loneliness, and in which people can begin to discover something of the fuller life of the church. Emilie, leader of the Trinity Voices choir, describes the feeling she gets when her choir hits a perfect harmony, a feeling of pride and deep connection with her community.

Once connections are made, there are other spaces and activities into which people can be invited, opportunities to get more deeply involved in this community and discover more of the gospel that animates it. One person might be invited to the fortnightly 'Inspire' group for mums, where babies and toddlers are looked after so that the mums have time to read the Bible together, and to discuss their questions about Christian faith. Another person might be ready to join an Alpha group, and discover more about what following Jesus involves. And once people are more involved, there are other opportunities for fellowship, teaching, and exploration of the faith.

Meeting, inviting, taking time

These are just a few of the elements of Trinity's varied and thriving witness, but they illustrate its nature well. First, eating together and making music together are powerful activities in people's lives. They energise and shape people, and involve them in a web of relationships. Trinity's witness meets people right in the midst of these sites of ordinary human intensity.

Second, those who come into these spaces are invited to continue on a journey toward deeper relationship and fuller involvement. The church's website says that 'we long to see people progress in their journey and become fully devoted followers of Jesus Christ who see themselves at the heart of God's people at Trinity.' The café and choirs are spaces in which the Trinity community says to those around them 'come and see, come and feel, come and share, the love that we have found'. Jules and others at Trinity then look for ways to build 'stepping stones' – spaces and activities like the 'Inspire' group, that allow people to move further along this journey into discipleship.

Third, this is an approach to witness that is willing to take time with people. This might start with a visitor venturing beyond Café12/31 into the main body of the church for a few minutes; it might involve a visitor having a chat with someone who shows a real interest in them; it might take the form of someone singing for the first time in one of the church's choirs. However it begins, the invitation to explore further is always there, but it is gentle, and it is different for each person, responding to the particular gifts, needs, interests and expectations that each person brings with them.

Witnessing in the power of the Spirit

There are many other projects and forms of witness in the life of Trinity. When we spoke to Jules, she said that she couldn't possibly tell us about them all in one meeting; there was simply too much going on. They are all, however, held together by the sense that this is a community on a journey together, united by a belief in God's power to change lives and relationships, and by a belief that this power works in and through them. Each person within the community is being called by God's Spirit on a journey deeper into knowledge of God, deeper into relationship with one another, and deeper into engagement with the surrounding world. The whole church community is being called by God's Spirit on a journey together, discovering what each new participant in its life can bring.

Sustaining all of this activity is a lot of work, and Jules doesn't think it likely that she will run out of things to do any time soon. A significant amount of energy is demanded. Nevertheless, Steve, the Rector, is clear that the energy needed for all this work comes from the Spirit. God is the one who leads people on this journey, by the Spirit; God is the one who draws people into relationship, by the same Spirit. All of this work flows from the attempt to discern what God wants to do in this place, and to respond to what God is already doing. It is, fundamentally, Jesus who meets people, Jesus who invites people to find in him the security, joy, friendship and adventure for which we have all been made, and Jesus who takes time with all the people of Lewes. And it is Jesus who commissions the people of Trinity Church to participate in his work, and gives them the Spirit to enable that participation.

3: Piccadilly

St James's Piccadilly is a church right in the midst of central London. From the busy street where Londoners, tourists, shoppers, office workers, and homeless people go about their lives, St James's gates open up on to a courtyard filled with the Piccadilly Market and a garden open to the public. Many languages can be heard amongst the stall holders and customers, as Union Jack bunting flutters over their heads; people come here to eat their lunch, meet with friends, and strike up conversations with strangers.

Spaces for witness

Tucked into a corner, not centre stage but still clearly visible, is a green shepherd's hut which houses the Counselling Caravan Drop-in. The counselling happens in partnership with a local college, and St James's provides the space. This is typical of their approach to witness, which often involves creating and providing space in many different ways, in partnership with others.

There is space for counselling; space for local business and creativity; space for connecting with nature and with other people. Space for concerts, at lunch time or in the evenings. Space for art installations which raise questions, highlight issues, and generate conversations. Space for homeless people to sleep safely during the day. Space to have profound encounters and challenging conversations. Space to celebrate and have fun. Space to be both host and guest. Space to learn new things. These are all different ways of expressing God's attentiveness and loving care.

The work of witness at St James's takes a whole variety of different forms. They run a breakfast, for instance, for people in the asylum system and people with no recourse to public funds. They have invested in creating a community garden, and collaborated with local scientists to create events educating people in ecological concerns. (They were the first urban church to receive the Eco Church Gold Award 'for care of God's earth in everyday work and witness', from A Rocha UK.) They are perhaps best known, however, for what the Rector, Lucy Winkett, calls 'liturgical advocacy'.

Liturgical advocacy

Sometimes this takes the form of art installations that make the headlines and are visited and discussed by large numbers of people. In 2018, for example, St James's collaborated with artist Arabella Dorman, to create an installation called 'Suspended'. Taking place over Christmas, the piece saw seven hundred pieces of clothing salvaged from Lesbos, animated with wire, to represent the people who wore them, and suspended in the roof of the nave. The message was that the people who are in refugee camps across Europe are suspended. They can't go back because it's not safe and they can't go forward because nobody's taking them, so their lives are being wasted. Lucy says, 'At the festival where we celebrate God becoming human, that is scandalous, and more than that, blasphemous. So it was a kind of a cry of protest against what was happening, and linking that to Christmas.'

These projects are political and can provoke strong reactions, negative and positive, but the aim is not to be controversial for the sake of notoriety. It is important for the team that the artwork is 'theologically literate' and 'liturgically based', rooted in something that the church is already celebrating. And it is important that it is grounded in, and accompanied by, pastoral encounter. They want to make sure that they're not just doing something like Suspended and then running away. They are meeting and talking to people who are in the situation about which they are speaking. Lucy says that they always aim for that kind of level of authenticity about what they are doing. In the case of 'Suspended', for instance, several of the congregation have volunteered for work amongst migrants on Lesbos, as well as in other locations.

Witness is not spectacle. The clothes suspended from the ceiling were real clothes, worn by real people, the fates of whom are unknown, some of whom will have died. The focus is on the injustice, the scandalous suffering of human beings created in God's image – and on the hope of the kingdom of God. For St James's, the test of whether a project like this is actually witness is whether 'it draw us out and point us to something else.'

'Bethlehem Unwrapped', another installation put in place around Christmas time, arose out of a parish pilgrimage to the Holy Land, including time spent in Bethlehem experiencing the security wall there between Palestinian and Israeli territory. It was jarring for the St James's pilgrims to witness how the

Israeli–Palestinian conflict has affected the situation on the ground in cities like Bethlehem, and then to come home to Christmas celebrations in which the town appears only in a storybook form. The project involved the creation of an exact replica of a Bethlehem segment of the wall across the church courtyard – and it was important to the team that, if visitors said it was an exaggeration, they were able to say, 'I've seen it and it looks like this.'

The team consulted with a wide range of people, including Israeli, Palestinian, and Druze groups, and held consultation meetings with the Israeli embassy and Board of Deputies before the event. The installation did nevertheless cause considerable controversy, particularly amongst some members of the Jewish community – but although the controversy risked damaging St. James's interfaith witness, it eventually had the opposite effect: new avenues of dialogue opened up between St James's and some parts of the Jewish community, resulting in greater understanding and mutual respect. Indeed, the wall was built so that at the end of a festival of cultural sharing two sections could be lowered down to form a bridge – witnessing to a different possibility.

Dropping anchors

Situated as it is in central London, St James's is a gathered congregation, and it is a particularly publicly visible church. With its access to people from so many different locations, and so many walks of life, a lot of St James's witness aims to speak into the 'greater conversation that the church must have with society.' The church is unusual in having an outside pulpit, added to the Christopher Wren building in the early twentieth century to give a particularly loud-voiced rector a platform to preach from. No longer used for sermons, that pulpit nevertheless provides a helpful image. Lucy notes that, in nautical usage, a 'pulpit' on a boat is 'the place you lean out from in order to drop the anchor more deeply.... So what we want to be doing in our witnessing is, in a way that people walking up and down Piccadilly can understand ... to be inviting them to drop their anchor, more deeply, into the spiritual life.' They want to 'create witnesses, to take people to places, and to help them face things' – to invite people to see the world as God sees it, to recognize the injustice that mars it, and from that place of encounter, to hear proclaimed the love and justice and peace of the kingdom of God.

4: Brancepeth

To reach St Brandon's church, you go through the castle gates at one end of
Brancepeth's main street. The church is tucked behind a screen of trees in the
castle grounds, but visitors to the castle's craft fairs or to its coffee shop often
find it. Passing the trees, they see in front of them a medieval church building
of honey-coloured stone, set in a grassy churchyard – and because the wooden
porch doors are normally unlocked, many of them go in. Not many are
expecting what they find inside.

The fire

One night in September 1998, a fire turned the church's rich seventeenth-
century panelling, its ornate screen and choir stalls, its box pews and altar,
to ash; it splintered the marble monuments, smashed the windows, and tore
down the roof. All that remained was a stone shell – and the brass eagle lectern,
adrift in a sea of rubble.

The fire was a traumatic disturbance in the life of the worshipping community.
It destroyed their memories and carefully tended heritage; it displaced them
to the village hall; it forced them to re-evaluate their purpose and identity.
Those who shared the church's journey through that time testify to the pain –
but they also testify that, far from scattering them, the process of responding
together to the fire made them more united and more collaborative, and more
determined than ever that the story of their community and of their building
should be a witness to Jesus' resurrection life.

The space that people enter now is the result of a long, slow process of
reconstruction and rededication, both for the building and for the community
that worships there. After the trauma of the fire, it took seven years before
the reconsecrated building could open for worship – and when it did re-open,
it was with a celebration of the eucharist and a renewal of the congregation's
baptismal vows.

The story of the building

The main thing that people notice as they come through the porch doors now
is the light. The building is open and airy, plain glass in most of the windows

letting light stream in. The space is uncluttered, the lines clean, the colours soft. The visitors' book is full of hundreds of messages saying things like 'A beautiful church, peaceful and bright'; 'A feeling of serenity as soon as we entered'; 'A holy place full of God's love'; and 'Thank you for keeping your doors open!'

The building is designed to tell a story. A line runs from west to east: there is an octagon of limestone around the base of the font at the west end; it is mirrored by two more, beneath the nave altar at the crossing and beneath the high altar at the east end. The east window – the only stained glass in the building – is bold and bright: the 'paradise window', depicting a burst of glorious flowers. This line from west to east starts from baptism and the beginning of the life of faith; it runs through the sites where that life is sustained week by week in the eucharist – and it runs on towards the hope of heaven and the light of glory. And out beyond the east window, the line finishes in a new Circle of Remembrance, where ashes are interred, awaiting the resurrection. Corbels supporting the roof trusses reinforce this story: from west to east, they represent birth, baptism, confirmation, marriage, family, prayer, death – and resurrection.

Visitors need help to read this story, and recently the PCC placed signs around the building, interpreting its parts. They are temporary at present, but the PCC hopes to make them permanent. A sign by the font, for instance, tells visitors that 'for hundreds of years children and adults have been baptized with water in this ancient font. The water represents new life – being washed, starting afresh, no longer being trapped by the things in our life that get in the way of our relationship with God. Christians believe that all this is possible through Jesus Christ.' Another, by the nave altar, reads 'The altar is the table at which Christians share communion: a wafer of bread, a sip of wine. It's that simple, but it is at the heart of what Christians believe. Knowing He would be crucified, Jesus shared bread and wine with His friends, telling them that the bread was His body broken for them, the wine His blood shed for them. This, His life, was His gift of love to them and all humanity. He asked that this be remembered every time anyone came to this table to share communion.' These signs – and there are several more – point visitors to the story of the Christian faith.

Welcome and community

The community that worships in this re-made building aims to make it a place of welcome. The doors are always open during the day, and visitors and villagers are invited to make use of the space – to come in simply from curiosity; for concerts and village events; for services at the major festivals; for baptisms, weddings, and funerals; for Messy Church; or for the parish eucharist services held every Sunday morning. Many more people from the village and the surrounding countryside come through the church's doors from time to time than appear on a typical Sunday morning, and many of them regard it firmly as their church. Asked recently what they most value about their church, members of the congregation spoke warmly of this welcome – though they also talked about their desire to extend it further, and to find ways not just of welcoming more people in, but of reaching out more intentionally into the wider community.

The other main note struck in people's description of what they value was the sense of community at St Brandon's. Nearly everyone who attends worship with any regularity gets actively involved – in everything from coffee rotas to preaching, pastoral visiting to flower arranging, Youth Group leading to bell-ringing. A welcome into the building, and into the worship that takes place there, quickly becomes a welcome to participate – to share in this life and become a part of it, drawing on whatever gifts a person brings with them. This invitation to participate in the life of this place, the life that takes place on the journey from baptismal font to paradise window, is at the heart of St Brandon's witness.

Anna Brooker, the recently arrived Priest in Charge, says, 'As a recent arrival, I am captivated by the story of St Brandon and by St Brandon's. Just as the saint over-came fear and storms to discover new lands, God has guided his people here, from a fearful loss to new life and purpose. As the beautiful building makes clear, we are on a journey, the cross of Christ before us and the Spirit's wind in our sails.'

Death and resurrection

One of the signs that help visitors read the building's story points them to something high on the wall above the chancel arch. 'The cross is at the heart of the Christian faith', it says. 'Through Jesus' death on the cross and rising to new life, God absorbs all the pain and darkness of the world and in us and gives us the freedom to experience true fullness of life. Our cross above the nave altar is made from timbers charred by the fire that almost destroyed the church; it shows that new hope springs up even in the depths of loss.' This building, and the people who worship in it, witness to the story of death and resurrection.

5. Walsall

St Gabriel's church stands in the midst of southern Walsall's changing social landscape. It is in a leafy suburb neighbouring a large social housing estate. It lies on the boundary between white working-class communities to the south and a more racially and socially diverse community to the north, bisected by the M6 motorway. The white working-class population is ageing and shrinking; the Asian British population is growing. The religious mix is changing too: there are five mosques and two temples, and the parish is now three-quarters Muslim; at Palfrey Junior School, about a mile from the church, nine out of ten pupils are Muslim. These changes have not always been welcomed, however, and have sometimes been met with hostility and discrimination.

St Gabriel's is an Anglo-Catholic church within the diocese of Lichfield, and is one of the ninety-six parishes under the extended care of the See of Ebbsfleet. Its largely ageing, white working-class congregation has in recent years been joined by Eastern European and African-Caribbean families and others. With the help of Father Mark McIntyre, who has been the parish priest for eight years, the church faces the question of what witness can mean in the midst of Walsall's religious diversity, and in relation to the tensions that sometimes surround it.

The church–mosque partnership

It is in this context that a church–mosque partnership emerged some four years ago. The initial idea did not come from the church. The Council Diversity Officer, himself a Muslim, came to the church brunch club to talk about the council's work, and in the course of the discussion suggested that the church might partner with a local Islamic community. He was also the one who identified the nearby Aisha Mosque as a possible partner.

What resulted was not a grand strategy, nor a dramatic development, but a slowly growing network of relationships. First, a group from St Gabriel's was invited to visit the mosque, and a small delegation of ten to fifteen went. They were warmly welcomed with food – something that was to become a regular feature of later encounters. They heard public recitation from the Qur'an with an explanation of what was read, and Fr Mark was invited to speak in the mosque's social area. Two months after this first visit, a mosque group came to visit the church, and a series of reciprocal visits began.

The connections and relationships made possible by these visits have created unexpected possibilities. Recently, for instance, a group of a dozen men and women came from the mosque in the wake of the attacks on Christians in Sri Lanka, saying that 'We want to stand in solidarity'. This local response to international events echoed the actions of the previous imam's family, who had protected churches in Egypt during the Morsi presidency when some Christian communities had been under threat. The mosque delegation came just before the beginning of Ramadan, and they came in for the start of Mass. The church presented the visitors with trays of dates for breaking fast during Ramadan.

The local hospice next to the church, Acorns Children's Hospice in the Black Country, is in some ways a microcosm of the parish. It is a ten-bed hospice specialising in children's end of life care and long-term life-threatening cases. Its patients are Eastern European, Asian British, and White British. There are shared prayers in the hospice across the different traditions. Funerals will be specific to a particular tradition, but when prayers are needed the call goes out to 'the nearest holy man' – so Fr Mark has, for example, been called out to pray with a Sikh family.

To give another example: Fr Mark's parents died recently. His mother died on Pentecost Sunday, which was during Ramadan. A friend from another mosque said he would pray for Fr Mark's mother at Iftar (the breaking of the fast after sunset during the Muslim holy month of Ramadan). Others at the mosque, when they learned of his parents' death, offered prayer for them too. They offered prayers 'for the death of a righteous person'. 'Our brother Fr Mark is grieving, and so are we.'

The local council (whose councillors are predominantly Muslim) has continued to play an important role in helping the different religious communities engage with each other. They have hosted meetings; they have listened; they have made suggestions. Other civic bodies are also involved: there is, for example, an English class run twice per week in the church organised and paid for by 'One Walsall', who support the voluntary sector in the local area. A complex web of partnerships and relationships is emerging.

Emerging relationships

The emergence of these relationship has not always been easy. There has sometimes been tension, sometimes misunderstanding, sometimes disagreement, and sometimes nervousness. On one occasion, for instance, during a Lent group, someone worried that 'There'll be a minaret on this church soon'. Nevertheless, the encounters continue. People from the church and the mosque meet to share food; they meet for theological exploration (to discuss prayer, for instance); and they collaborate in social action (the church, for example, collecting items for the mosque's food bank). A network of relationships, engagement, and co-operation has emerged – strands that help bind together the wider community.

Transforming Communities Together, an initiative established by the Diocese of Lichfield and the Church Urban Fund Together network in 2014, identified St Gabriel's as a model to encourage other partnerships. There are now three active partnerships in Walsall, and three in Wolverhampton, including Anglican–Muslim and Methodist–Muslim links. Ray Gaston, who serves as Interfaith Enabler and Bishop's Adviser for the Wolverhampton episcopal area, has suggested that 'Church–Mosque Partnerships' could be formally recognised as an element of the diocese's work.

The congregation in St Gabriel's is changing, and Walsall itself is changing. The church and the mosque are adapting to changing circumstances, in a partnership with a strong dimension of social action. The imagination and energy for such partnership springs from local leaders who are themselves religious but whose authority and influence derives from their civic office rather than religious position. It is a complex mix of overlapping interests, institutions, and identities.

In this context, God's action is visible in the emergence of relationships – the building of peace in a context of tension, and of connection in a context of fragmentation. It is visible in the church's partnership with the mosque; it is visible in the local council's relationship with the church, the mosque, and local religious communities; it is visible in a white working-class parish adapting to life together with Asian communities that are now a significant local majority; it is visible in reciprocal local responses to international events that threaten minorities. But most of all, perhaps, it is visible in a network of local communities, on a small scale, within and across religious traditions, in which ordinary people seek to pursue decent lives, to live with their differences, to feed the hungry, to pray for one another, to support grieving families. Little of this is the result of strategic planning. The Spirit truly blows where it will, and this work has been more a matter of responding to opportunities as they arise, pursuing the possibility of deeper relationship wherever it appears. In their participation in this activity, the people of St Gabriel's are witnessing to the God of peace.

6: Manchester Chaplaincy

On 22nd May 2017, Manchester Arena was bombed in a terrorist attack after a concert by the singer Ariana Grande. Twenty-three people were killed (including the bomber) and many more were injured. It was an event which threw the city of Manchester into shock and mourning, especially affecting its young people, many of whom were at the concert. What is the appropriate shape of Christian witness in the face of grief, incomprehension, and questioning about God?

This question resonated at St Peter's House, the Christian chaplaincy serving the Universities of Manchester, the Royal Northern College of Music, and the University of Law, together forming the largest student community in the UK, with some 80,000 students.

A new charity was established in 2017 to oversee the ecumenical chaplaincy, with a new team of women and men under the leadership of Ben Edson and Hannah Skinner working to discover how chaplaincy might work in this place. That work has involved them in paying close attention to their locality, to the challenges and possibilities that it presents, and to the particular resources that the chaplaincy team have available.

The new team found inspiration, for instance, in a symbol of Manchester itself: the worker bee. Bee symbols appear across the city on pavements and on bollards, and in the summer of 2018 there was a public art project in which over 120 six-foot-high bees were installed across the city. The bees were designed and created by different artists, and the chaplaincy commissioned their own multi-faith bee, 'The Love Bee', to be a symbol of their work. Ben was already himself a beekeeper, and Manchester Art Gallery offered him two beehives and colonies to work with. The chaplaincy team drew on this local symbol of Manchester's hard work and industry, on Ben's own practical experience of bee-keeping, and on the biblical metaphor of honey with all its associations of sustenance and sweetness – and bees and bee-keeping have become for them a central picture of what it means to pay attention to, celebrate, and interpret to others God's activity here in Manchester. Bee-language now abounds, an old bee hive is now utilised as a prayer station with people being invited to 'Tell the Bees', and a café has been opened called Milk and Honey.

Attention, invitation, and connection

The team's work of witness involves *catching people's attention*. In October 2017, for instance, the team ran a publicity campaign using the message 'Just watch us' – a message designed to get people talking, to spark curiosity, and to encourage people to ask questions about the chaplaincy and what it might be about.

Curiosity is important as a value for the chaplaincy. University is about learning new things and encountering difference. The team sees its role being to evoke curiosity and open possibilities. When minds are opened through curiosity, people become more open to the encounter with God. The chaplaincy has seen a massive increase in footfall as a result of this emphasis on curiosity – on saying, as openly as possible, 'Come and see!'

The chaplaincy team have worked to invite people in, removing physical barriers, enabling people to see inside the chaplaincy building, making it easier for people to cross thresholds, and changing the whole appearance and perception of the place from obstacle to encouragement. They have worked to make the chaplaincy building a place of hospitality and welcome, to be good hosts. At the same time, they have worked at being good guests. The Iona invitation to communion notes that Jesus 'was always the guest' and this has illuminated the team's understanding of Christian witness. They understand themselves as being the guests of the universities, and have worked to understand what it means to be good guests in an institutional context where they have no structural or institutional authority.

Whether as hosts or guests, the team work at making connections. Students often socialise, work and live primarily with other students, meaning that they do not necessarily connect with the wider city of Manchester. The chaplaincy has become a place for making such connections with people across the city, for the common good of the city, and to enable people to find God at work in the encounters that the chaplaincy facilitates. Through their volunteer programme students work alongside one another and alongside people who have experienced homelessness, people from other cultures, and people who are living with disabilities. The chaplaincy hosts a variety of organisations such as a charity that works with young people to prevent homelessness, an agency that encourages access to higher education, and a centre for international women artists. Downstairs, the team have developed a hub to assist social entrepreneurs needing help with start-up. There is a wholeness studio offering yoga instruction, Pilates, and mindfulness. Staff and students in need of pastoral support or counselling are discovering that St Peter's House offers that gift.

One connection that is important to the life of the chaplaincy but not visible in the foreground of its work is its connection to the worshipping life of the church. St. Peter's House was originally St Peter's church *and* chaplaincy – but now it is simply the chaplaincy. St Peter's church is, however, still a place of worship and witness, and it provides a core which nourishes the wider work of the chaplaincy through prayer, even if it is not the place where those who encounter the chaplaincy are typically expected to end up. Nevertheless, the fact that the chaplaincy is supported by a worshipping community has meant that many of the people amongst whom they work do in fact come looking for church – and one of the lessons the team has drawn from this is that loosening the connections to the church can sometimes help lead people back to church.

Everything is connected

Witness means creating those worker bee connections, pollinating, working together and creating nourishing honey for physical and spiritual health. It is sometimes slow and faltering work: there are still places in student life where there is no conversation and the team has had to learn to walk alongside those who remain cut off and wait for the right time, God's time. Nevertheless, opportunities continually arise.

Above all, the chaplaincy aims to connect with the specific needs of the place and time in which they find themselves. They discovered, for instance, that a secular university really does want to engage with the idea of peace, and this was critical after the bombing. The aftermath created an opportunity to talk about peace, and to point towards what God is doing in the world, especially when people were asking questions about good, evil, hatred, and peace.

Hannah says, 'We've developed a simple but challenging vision: "Everything is Connected", believing that God is at work before us all in all things and that our task is to journey with people as they explore what this may mean. We recognise that people, place, spirituality, well-being and the search for understanding interweave, and that everything flourishes when one thing leads to another and back again!'

7: Manchester Cathedral

Manchester Cathedral sits on the banks of the Irwell, between Manchester Victoria and the Arndale Shopping Centre, the Corn Exchange and the National Football Museum. A distinctive presence surrounded by shops, restaurants, and offices, it stands at the heart of the city, and of the wider city region. The cathedral's witness grows out of this distinctive location, according to the Dean, Rogers Govender. Under his leadership, the cathedral aims as much as possible to be a space that is not closed off from the city, nor protected from the bustle of the wider world surrounding it, but open to it, and welcoming to it. Rogers wants all the people of the Greater Manchester region to recognise this as their cathedral.

A sign of hope

'Our vision', he says, 'is to grow, build community and make a difference in our society and wider world through the good news of our Lord Jesus Christ. We seek to live out our faith in God in practical ways and to be an inclusive Cathedral as we see the grace of God at work around us.'[14] His way of pursuing that vision grows out of his experience in South Africa, where he campaigned against apartheid in the midst of a deeply divided society. In such a context, the church needed to be called to stand against that division: it needed to be a sign of the kingdom of God, in which distinctions of race, culture, and wealth would not separate people. The church can be, and has to be, a witness to the new humanity that God is creating in Jesus.

That lesson is no less true in the UK than it was in South Africa. The cathedral stands in the midst of a society that very easily polarises over responses to terrorism, over the activity of the far right, over Brexit. In such a context, the cathedral tries to be a sign of God's welcome, a sign of God's inclusive love, a sign of God's delight in the diversity of humanity. It seeks to be a sign of hope in the midst of a fractured world.

The power to convene

The Dean has discovered that the cathedral in general, and his office in particular, have tremendous power to convene and to host: an in-built soft power that it is possible to harness and use for the common good. That power shows itself in numerous concrete ways. Rogers was, for instance, approached by the new Chief Constable several years ago, and asked what the Cathedral could do to help the city address the thousands of hate crime incidents that disfigure its life each year. Since then, he has convened the Challenging Hate Forum, bringing together leaders from several different faith communities and people from the police, the fire service, community groups and the Town Hall, each month, often in the cathedral. The Forum meets to reflect on aspects of hate crime affecting the city, and encourages its participants to share information with their communities with a view to raising awareness.

The relationships developed in the midst of that work have proved fruitful in other ways. For example, in 2016, soon after the attacks in Paris, the Dean was approached by a Muslim colleague worried by the rise of Islamophobia. In response, the cathedral helped to organise the first of what has become an annual 'Peace and Unity' event. Most recently, in 2018, that event brought together more than three hundred people from across the city.

Many other forms of working and learning together have emerged from the network of relationships generated by this work. An inter-faith climate crisis group, 'Our Faith, Our Planet'; a vigil held a week after the Sri Lanka bombings at Easter in 2019, bringing together Christians, Muslims, Hindus and Buddhists; an inter-faith youth Iftar held in the cathedral, and focused on encouraging young people into community leadership and service across the city – the list of activities, events, and relationships is long, and growing.

Opening the building

All of this is made possible because of where the cathedral stands, and that is true in ways that go far beyond the literal. The cathedral building, in its city-centre location, stands for something. It is a building that has a particular history, explained to tourists and other visitors by guides, in leaflets, and on explanatory panels. And, shaped, filled, and coloured by that history, it is a building that tells a particular story: a story of faith in the God who, in Jesus, breaks down dividing walls, and who welcomes all into loving fellowship. It is a building that stands for a particular kind of welcoming, inclusive life.

Some are attracted to the building out of curiosity, or the desire to explore. Some come inside when the cathedral nave is hired out as an events space. Some come in when they come to any of the inter-faith and cultural events that the cathedral hosts. All kinds of people, from all sorts of backgrounds and with all manner of attitudes and expectations, come in, and the Dean seeks to ensure that this building is as open to them as possible, and that the threshold to entry, the barriers to visitors feeling welcomed and at home in this place, are as low as possible.

Two or three times each year, the cathedral holds invitation Sundays, welcoming back people who have been baptised, and their friends and families, when they have lost touch with church. The idea is to attract them back again, over the threshold, and to make it clear that this church is not simply a club for its regular members. Here, too, the Dean's aim is to lower barriers to participation, and to diminish the extent to which people need to know the rules before they feel they can join in. Having worked in this and other ways to open the doors and lower the threshold, the cathedral has seen the numbers of those worshipping more than triple.

The cathedral is firmly a place of prayer and praise, and of beauty dedicated to God. All of that worship, prayer, and beauty shapes the space that is thrown open to all of these guests, friends, and visitors – and the Dean ensures that none of the events damages that ongoing worshipping life. This life is what gives the building its atmosphere and character; it is what makes it something other than a neutral venue.

Rogers has found that many of the people who come through the cathedral recognise this, and see its importance. One token of this is the way in which donations from beyond the worshipping Christian community have come in for the upkeep and enhancement of the building – a new organ, for instance, and a new stained-glass window speaking of 'Hope'. People recognise that this space is a resource for the whole community, but that it is so because of rather than despite its specific Christian identity.

The cathedral's life of worship is not, either physically or in other ways, separated from the other events, the other forms of witness that go on within it. The boundary between worship and witness is deliberately porous; Rogers hopes that both worshippers in the cathedral's regular round of services, and all those who find themselves in the cathedral for other reasons, find it simply natural that a building dedicated to the God of Jesus Christ will also be a building dedicated to peace, to inclusion, to the building of bridges, and to the overcoming of division and hatred. The building is a sign of God's kingdom, interpreted by all the activity that takes place within it.

8: Bethnal Green

Walk down Bethnal Green Road from the tube station and both the light and shadow side of east London life is spread out around you. Young professionals going home in smart suits pass homeless people sitting in doorways. Groups of young people stand around chatting and talking on phones, while mothers push their children past the pubs and fast food outlets. Joggers dodge the traffic; people in hats, hairbands and headscarves wait patiently at the lights. Further up, in Columbia Road, home of the famous flower market, local people and visitors sample art galleries, vintage-clothing stores, and cafés.

St Peter's has been at the heart of the area since the 1840s, but by 2010 its congregation was dwindling – until the new parish priest, Adam Atkinson, working with Heather Atkinson (who has now become Vicar) entered into a church planting partnership with St Paul's Shadwell to bring twenty new people to the church and begin a new chapter. That began a process that has now seen the congregation increase to more than one hundred.

Waking and dreaming

The first task of witness was simply to wake up the building: to open the doors and turn the lights back on, creating a visible sense of openness and activity. Heather remarks on the 'easy wins' – buying a decent vacuum cleaner, raising the height of a table, providing heating and blankets.

The second task was to begin dreaming dreams about what the church could be. This meant learning from those who had been associated with the church for a long time – people who knew its heritage and its traditions. It meant learning in particular from people with mental illness and older people with dementia, who challenged easy visions of what the church might become. It meant trying to be faithful to the tradition of the place, while finding ways to inhabit that tradition in accessible and energising ways. In a striking phrase, one of the churchwardens, Andy, talks about what is now happening as being the answer to the prayers of previous generations who had loved the church. To see oneself as answer to prayer brings huge hope, but also huge responsibility: 'pews have memories'.

Prayer and worship

Prayer is the foundation on which all of St Peter's witness rests. The chancel is a prayer space; other spaces are turned into oases of prayer. The porch is a place of 'say one for me', and people enter the church precincts through words of prayer: there was a local school competition to design new gates with wording from Psalm 24. The parish is walked and prayed over continually.

Worship is the soil in which witness grows. St Peter's now identifies as a place where people can 'worship God, make friends and change the world'. St Peter's has become a cross-tradition church, with different forms of worship sitting comfortably alongside one another. There is a Sung Eucharist at 10am and a service with children's groups at 11am, and a period of shared coffee and notices mixing the two congregations in between.

Noticing and celebrating

On the basis of that prayer and worship, St Peter's Christian witness involves *noticing what is going on in the community* and discovering how to connect with it. St Peter's has a small staff team but many volunteers, and has instituted listening campaigns and what Adam calls a 'laboratory' in which creative ways of engaging with the community can flourish. When the local pub, The Birdcage, was taken under new ownership, for instance, Adam looked for birds in Scripture and blessed the new endeavour. The church makes a deliberate attempt to find links between their faith and everyday happenings in the community that impact people's lives.

Another important aspect of St Peter's Christian witness is *celebration*. The parish has 'heart-to heart' parties, celebrations in cafés, and on the street. Adam says it is important to remember that every street is important and has a group of people who worship Jesus. Together with Citizens UK, the church listened to the community's needs and helped to get a zebra crossing on a dangerous road. Afterwards, everyone danced across it in celebration. Building relationships of joy allows a direct witness to God's action in the world.

Another wonderful example of celebration is the collaboration with the charity SPEAR, which works to get young people into employment. After a six-week course, the young people come to be applauded and celebrated by the SPEAR coaches and by the church. The young people, many of whom struggle with confidence or mental health issues, are encouraged and cheered, their journey forward crowned with whoops and celebrated with wine. They are offered the chance to feel that their lives and achievements matter, even if it is only saying 'thank you for listening' in front of an audience.

Bringing the gospel into the heart of the community

Despite the labour of love involved in hauling the piano to Columbia Road, the Christmas Carols event at the late-opening Advent markets is something that *everyone* mentions. Adam stands on the piano in a Santa hat and a dog collar, offering prayers, a collect, and blessings. Aesthetics are important, – the scent of Glühwein from The Royal Oak, the darkness, the joy, but also especially, in the midst of the hustle and bustle, the times of silence, generating conversations, confessions, first contacts and longing and desire for God. These are planned for, with prayer teams: the heart of the Christ story in he midst of Christmas consumerism. This is 'show and tell' Christianity, the essence of witness here. In 2017, the event reached four thousand people across four Wednesday markets.

Similarly, Palm Sunday is led by bagpipes gathering people into an open-air marquee for the gospel of the palms and the readings. Jesus arrives on the Green with a donkey. Holy Week comes out into the community to be seen by all.

Conversely, a particular aspect of witness at St Peter's has been the identification and acknowledgement of 'places of resistance'. There are some signals of 'don't come' which have to be acknowledged and understood. Christian witness is therefore about the long game, being prepared to wait, pray and exercise discernment. As both Adam and Heather say, some things are for today and others for tomorrow. There are dead ends and there are problems. Some creative ideas don't work and have to be relinquished and not regretted. Some things have been stopped. Money is an issue. The church does not have good kitchens or toilets. There are boundaries and limitations. Such things are prayed over, and then given over to God.

Heather, Adam and their family have poured a great deal into this vision of St Peter's, and the work has been costly for them. But they have certainly not worked alone. Surprising leaders have come forward. Peggy, knitting at a Life Group, has been a catalyst for others; Julie, aged eighty, has inspired and developed energy for witness in others. Both Adam and Heather pay tribute to the bravery of young people who gave a mission year to St Peter's. Witnessing is a matter of partnership, and partnership means not holding everything close but letting it go and trusting others – and, through and behind them, trusting God.

How are we going to respond?

Discussion: Reviewing the case studies

Where do you see similarities with your own church in the different contexts for witness in the eight case studies? Where do you see contrasts?

Where do you see similarities with your own church in the different approaches to witness taken in the eight case studies? Where do you see contrasts?

Where might you find affirmation here for how your church is serving as a witness?

Where might you find a challenge?

Reflection: Inhabit and imagine

Inhabit

Read through the case studies and pick one which especially inspires or intrigues you. What does that story offer your own situation? Perhaps you might like to visit the place of the case study yourself or talk further to the people involved in it. Start a dialogue or a friendship. How might your own church be inspired by the case study story to think about witness?

Imagine

What could you or your church do to be better witnesses in your own context? What would you most like to celebrate about where you are now? What resources might you need to change things, even a little?

Part 3: RESPONSES

In the words of Isaiah 41:20 that we quoted at the start of Part 1, we have told these stories 'so that all may see and know, all may consider and understand, that the hand of the Lord has done this'. They are intended as an encouragement and an inspiration, but also as a prompt to further thought – so that we can 'consider and understand' more of what it means to be called as God's witnesses.

We therefore finish with a series of responses, prompted by these stories, which point in some of the directions in which they might take our thinking. The first is from the working group that produced this report; the remainder are from people we invited to reflect on these stories from the perspective of their own involvement in witness.

1: The Theology of Witness

In response to these stories of witness, we can re-tell the story of God's action that provides their backdrop, and that helps us to see their significance.

God raises up witnesses to God's own life. Supremely, God raises up the true witness, Jesus of Nazareth, who communicates to us the life of God. And God sends the Holy Spirit to bear witness to Jesus with our spirits – teaching us to recognise and to welcome Jesus' witness.[15]

Jesus' witness is itself shaped by the Spirit. He is shaped by the witnesses whom God raised up before him (he is brought up by his faithful parents, he reads the Scriptures, he learns from the life of the synagogue and the temple). He is shaped by his engagement with those around him (responding to their needs, answering their questions).[16] He then in turn lives and speaks as a witness – God's perfect witness. He draws all people to himself, and by doing so draws them all to his Father.

God raises up witnesses to God's own life throughout creation, and throughout history. Those whose eyes are opened by the Spirit can see that the earth is full of the glory of God: 'Ever since the creation of the world his eternal power and divine nature, invisible though they are, have been understood and seen through the things he has made'. They can also learn to read 'the signs of the times'. They can learn to see God active in all manner of surprising characters – from the Persian king Cyrus to Balaam – and Balaam's donkey.[17]

It is in the midst of all these witnesses raised up by God that we should think about the church's witness – and understand the significance of the case studies described above. The church can witness only because it has seen and heard God's witness in Christ, and because it goes on seeing and hearing God at work in all the witnesses that God raises up. The church is always in the process of learning to witness – learning from God's witnesses. It doesn't initiate witness, or possess it. Instead, it is always held in circulating currents of witness – always receiving witness from others, and then passing on to others what it has received. (Think of Paul, telling the Corinthian church that 'I handed on to you as of first importance what I in turn had received' – the good news 'that Christ died for our sins in accordance with the scriptures' (1 Corinthians 15:3).

The church can witness only because God works in it by Word and Spirit, enabling the church to participate in God's work of witness.

The church itself is witness-shaped. It passes on witness in word and sacrament, which are witnesses raised up by God to lead us deeper into the mystery of Christ. It lives by the witness of all the saints and martyrs, each of whose lives show us more of the life of God. The members of the body show Christ to each other; each showing something different of the life of Christ – and we sometime face the difficulty of discerning that life in each other across our deep disagreements. We witness to each other across our ecumenical divides, and are slowly learning how to receive and celebrate that witness. We witness to the world in prophetic word and action, and in evangelism. And we learn to recognise the witnesses that God raises up outside the church, witnesses who prophesy to us and turn our hearts further towards God.

The church is constantly engaged in learning from all God's witnesses how to witness. We learn how to see God at work in the world, and we learn how to show what we have seen. The church's life is, therefore, a series of experiments in witness – the case studies above amongst them. Every disciple's life is a life of faithfully improvised witness. Witness is not an activity that starts in the church and flows outwards: it is a gloriously tangled ecology, tended by God, within which we can find our place.

2: Welcome, witness, and the work of the Spirit

Muthuraj Swamy, Director of the Cambridge Centre for Christianity Worldwide, writes:

This report is very enriching and encouraging. The reflections and the eight stories shared here are very insightful. As I have been reading the report, I have been pausing to relate the insights here to my own reflections on this theme.

Let me begin with my story of coming to Christianity. My becoming a Christian happened when I was seven years old, and it happened solely because the church I had a chance to go to witnessed to Christ in their everyday lives. I was casually invited as a friend by my friends and peers to join them for Sunday school in a nearby church. I started going with them. After noticing me there for a few weeks, on one Sunday during the Sunday school after the morning worship, the priest in the church told me he had seen me, and asked me if I was interested in going there regularly. I had to give an answer, 'Yes' or 'No', as I was standing in front of him, and the rest of the Sunday school students and teachers were sitting beside me. I did not have my parents there to ask. At that point, what flashed through my mind was how the church members used to talk to me, smile at me, say simple words of welcoming before and after the worship service. At that age, those actions and their lives pointed to me to what kind of God they were worshipping. I said to the priest that I would be happy to come to church regularly.

Acts 1:6-8 is a biblical text which quite often I turn to for reflecting on mission, evangelism, and witness. In this text, the disciples of Jesus find themselves still learning about Christ and his work, in spite of being his disciples for more than three years and after witnessing his life, teachings, death, and resurrection. When Jesus was just about to ascend into heaven, they ask him 'Lord, is this the time when you will restore the kingdom to Israel?' Jesus does not appreciate that question because it was completely misconceived, and tells them instead, 'You will receive power when the Holy Spirit has come upon you; and you will be *my witnesses* in Jerusalem, in all Judea and Samaria, and to the ends of the earth.' The emphasis on 'my' is important for me. As this report says, witnessing is primarily a response – a response to what God has done in Christ.

Whom the witnessing is pointing to and in whom a change is expected are important questions. The general notion is that we witness in order that other people change or must change. And most often this change is from wrong to right or from untruth to truth. But mission and evangelism built on such notions of witnessing have led to backlashes in the past and today. The most interesting thing about Jesus' disciples in this text is that they could not yet understand God's salvific will and plan for the whole world. They were asking questions about political power conditioned by their particular time and geographical context. But Jesus calls for a change. And the change that he demands is from his disciples. The change in the context of witnessing always begins from the one who witnesses.

The *Witness* report highlights that witnessing is a slow process. Indeed! Sadly, the issue of 'urgency' in mission has been there from the first century and pops up quite often. Slogans like 'converting the world in this generation' are prevalent in some Christian circles. But Jesus rebukes the disciples about their question about time. Witnessing needs to be empowered by God the Holy Spirit who is boundless and breaks all boundaries, connecting Judea, Samaria, and the ends of the earth – and when that happens 'communities of witnesses' become possible.

Dr Swamy co-edited with Stephen Spencer one of the volumes that were prepared for the (postponed) 2020 Lambeth Conference, dedicated to 'evangelism and witness'. The volume was published as Witnessing Together: Global Anglican Perspectives on Evangelism and Witness (*London: Forward Movement, 2019*). *The book contains reflections from a number of Anglican theologians and mission practitioners from different parts of the globe on the theme of witness.*

3: Witnessing through persistence in the face of difficulties

Hannah Lewis, Pioneer Minister with the Deaf Community, writes:

Responding from the perspective of a Deaf priest ministering with the Deaf community could take one of three directions: I could talk about witness from the hearing church to Deaf people – where the need to establish relationship and communication as a precursor to witnessing involves learning a whole new language and all the extra time and effort put in on both sides to reduce communication barriers. I could talk about the witness of Deaf people to each other, where Deaf people learn something new in BSL and instantly want to share it with others, where preaching is never just one way as conversations are held between preacher and congregation and among the congregation as to what exactly is meant.

But what I want to talk about is the witness of one Deaf congregation to the whole church – as well as to other Deaf people. This church witnesses to the faithfulness and the persistence of God simply by the fact it still exists. In its time – over 150 years or so – this oftentimes small group of believers has worshipped in at least five different locations and survived being uprooted by circumstance (and not by choice) five times. Service times and frequencies have changed, leaders, both internal and external, have come and gone. It has survived periods without the support of the diocese and without a priest who could communicate with them fluently in their own language. It has survived years of only half understanding what is being said 'up front', of being on the edges of the church, of meeting only once a month. And they are still there. People come and people go, sometimes it has been very small (double figures on a Sunday are rare) but they don't give up. They challenge the idea of 'success' on any terms – size, wealth, status. They are accepting, inclusive, and resilient. And they are still there – they point to God who is faithful, who isn't tied to one place or one time or one way of worshipping. They point to God who is there through the discrimination that they experience, through lack of understanding, through being Deaf in the hearing world. They point to God who brings the 'uplift' they need to get through the challenges of everyday life as Deaf BSL users in a sometimes hostile hearing world. They point to the importance of the Eucharist as a way to see and hear from God even when the words are inaccessible. When they are enabled to 'see and hear' in their own language and their understanding increases they are enabled to witness in words to the faithfulness of God that they have found. As one busy Reader who helps out once a month has said, 'I come to the Deaf church for a break, to be fed by their accepting, uncomplaining witness.'

It is important not to over-romanticize this witness – it doesn't take away from the absolute necessity for witness to and welcome of the Deaf community (by both Deaf and hearing people) in their own language of BSL. However, it is good to share to encourage others – you don't have to be big or busy to be able to point to God.

4: Evangelists as language teachers

Martyn Snow, Bishop of Leicester, writes:

I love hearing stories of churches responding with creativity and imagination as they seek to bear witness. And let's be clear, imagination and creativity are essential in a context where the majority are indifferent and have little idea of why the church even exists.

As Chair of the College of Archbishops' Evangelists, I am particularly interested in the role of evangelists in helping the whole church imagine a new way of engaging with a rapidly changing context. I believe that this will involve evangelists themselves re-examining their role and the whole church being ready to accept the gift of the evangelist.

The missiologist Stefan Paas, in his most recent book *Priests and Pilgrims,* explores our current context through the theme of exile: 'for a church that is expelled from the centre it is no longer possible to "speak from the clouds" … Instead, she will have to assume a *testimonial* voice… that is, not to point towards [herself], [her] own history and cultural superiority, but rather to expect everything from the coming Lord who has lived among us humbly and hidden, as a suffering servant.'[18]

This 'testimonial voice' runs as a thread through the examples in this document, examples of churches learning to speak a new language in a new land (or interpret old language for a new generation). So I observe a renewed emphasis on listening (essential for learning a new language), many small 'experiments' (trying out the new language), and simple story telling (learning any new language can feel like regressing to childhood!).

However, I would also want to emphasise that just as the church corporately must learn to speak in new tongues, so too individual Christians need to be equipped to bear witness in the varying contexts of their day-to-day lives – contexts which today include workplaces where it is forbidden to speak of personal faith or social media where devout Christians can expect ridicule. This calls for genuine personal courage as well as humility.

This is where evangelists can be a real gift to the wider church. Not the stereotypical speaker at a big event or TV celebrity, but people like Maureen who mentored me in an inner-city housing estate. Maureen visited people in their own homes and spoke of Jesus in such a natural and disarming way (her 'testimonial voice') that many were intrigued and wanted to know more. She had a very particular gift and calling, and part of this gift was to inspire courage in other Christians. They may not have her boldness or her ability to lead people to a point of expressing faith in community, but they were made to see that behind the indifference or the dismissive attitude of many, there is often a 'haunting', a sense that there must be something beyond the 'immanent frame' (to quote Charles Taylor).

I would argue that we need evangelists more than ever today if the church is to be fruitful in her witness. Pastors and teachers create community where the people of God are formed into the likeness of Christ and so become witnesses. Evangelists help that community to articulate faith in the language of the people they serve. Evangelists are the church's 'language teachers', encouraging us to speak no matter how diffident or unsure we feel (and recognising that this is a strength in our new context), and enabling each of us individually and the church corporately to find our 'testimonial voice'.

How are we going to respond?

Discussion: Witnessing where we are

Consider how you might go about producing a 'case study' about witness in your own church.

- What might be some of the activities on which you would want to focus?

- What might be some of the key themes you would want to bring out?

- Which biblical passages might you want to draw on?

- Who might you need to talk to in order to understand more fully how your church is witnessing?

Perhaps you would like to try writing this up after the discussion. Once you start, it may be hard to stop, so keeping it at no more than around 1,200 words (the rough length of the case studies in the report) might be helpful. You could use it on your church website or find other ways to share it.

You might also consider sharing it more widely. You could do that by contacting us through the designated page on the Church of England website, **www.churchofengland.org/witness**.

Tell us about what you want to do, pass on your own stories, and help us learn more about the fantastic examples of Christian witness which are shining out in the Church of England.

Reflection: Experiment

This report highlights the risks and sacrifices we sometimes have to take in order to follow God's call to us. What would you be prepared to risk or to dare to be better witnesses? How are you upholding the good news of God's love in your own situation? Where might you be inspired to start something new, restart something desired but not attempted? Who could help or be a partner?

_____

Notes

1. The Lambeth Conference 1930: Encyclical Letter from the Bishops with Resolutions and Reports (London: SPCK/New York: Macmillan, 1930), pp. 17–18.

2. The Church of England, 'The Revolution of God's Love', https://www.archbishopofcanterbury.org/priorities/evangelism-and-witness (accessed 11 December 2019).

3. Deuteronomy 6:4; Psalm 34:8; 1 John 1:1; 2 Corinthians 2:14; Isaiah 41:20.

4. Exodus 3:2–3.

5. Luke 24:2–5.

6. The Church of England, 'The Revolution of God's Love', https://www.archbishop ofcanterbury.org/priorities/evangelism-and-witness (accessed 11 December 2019).

7. Joshua 24:25–27.

8. John 6:2,15.

9. See, for example, Mark 8:29–30.

10. The descriptions in this paragraph are drawn from the 'five marks of mission'. See https://www.anglicancommunion.org/mission/marks-of-mission.aspx (accessed 11 Dec 2019).

11. The Lambeth Conference 1958, *The Encyclical Letter from the Bishops together with the Resolutions and Reports* (London: SPCK / Greenwich, CT: Seabury, 1958), I.26.

12. *Calling All God's People: A Theological Reflection on the Whole Church Serving God's Mission* (London: Church House Publishing, 2019). See also *Kingdom Calling* (London: Church House Publishing, 2020).

13. Nelle Morton, *The Journey is Home* (New York: Beacon Press, 1986), p. 205.

14. Rogers Govender, 'Welcome from the Dean', http://www.manchestercathedral.org (accessed 27 May 2019).

15. Revelation 3:14; Romans 8:16.

16. Luke 2:39–52.

17. Romans 1:20; Matthew 16:3; Isaiah 45; Numbers 22:21–39.

18. Stefan Paas, *Pilgrims and Priests: Christian Mission in a Post-Christian Society* (London: SCM, 2019), drawing on the work of Walter Brueggemann.